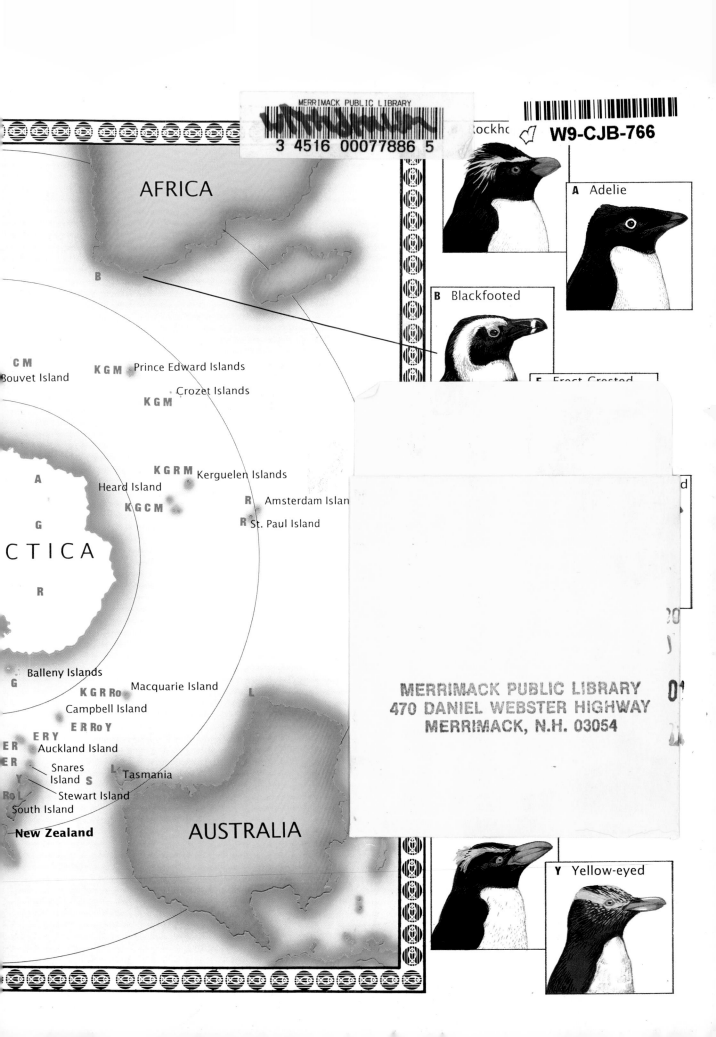

AFRICA

Rockho...

A Adelie

B Blackfooted

F Frost Crested

CM
Bouvet Island

KGM Prince Edward Islands

Crozet Islands

KGM

KGRM Kerguelen Islands

Heard Island

R Amsterdam Islan...

KGCM

R St. Paul Island

A

G

CTICA

R

Balleny Islands

G

KGRRo Macquarie Island

Campbell Island

ERRoY

ERY

ER Auckland Island

ER

Snares
Island S Tasmania

Y

RoL Stewart Island

South Island

New Zealand

AUSTRALIA

L

Y Yellow-eyed

CATHERINE PALADINO

POMONA

THE BIRTH OF A PENGUIN

A New England Aquarium Book

FRANKLIN WATTS

New York • London • Toronto • Sydney

1991

ACKNOWLEDGMENTS

With special thanks to Dan Laughlin, Supervisor of Aquarists, whose commitment and expertise have made the New England Aquarium's penguin-rearing program a success, and whose helpful advice made this book possible; to our dedicated team of aquarists: Holly Martel, Heather Urquhart, Chris Gaquin, Paula Dolan, Lucy Keith, and Nancy Etheridge for their invaluable contribution to the story and photographs; to the many volunteers who have helped care for our penguins; to Senior Publicist Andrea Conley, for her valued assistance in the penguin pool; and to Greg Early, Associate Curator of Animal Care, whose patience and skill enabled us to share in a penguin's life story from its beginning.

EDITOR'S NOTE:

This is a true-to-life account of the early life of a blackfooted penguin. However, several blackfooted penguins served as models for the photographs used in this book.

Diagram by James Needham

Pages 1, 15, 23, 24, 25: photographs copyright © 1990 New England Aquarium by Michael DeMocker; pages 9, 10 bottom, 13, 14, 16, 17: photographs copyright © New England Aquarium by Kenneth Mallory; page 21 left: photograph copyright © Dennis Stierer; page 28: photograph copyright © Animals Animals/A. Bannister; other photographs copyright © New England Aquarium by Catherine Paladino.

Library of Congress Cataloging-in-Publication Data

Paladino, Catherine.
Pomona : the birth of a penguin / Catherine Paladino.
p.   cm.
"A New England Aquarium book."
Includes bibliographical references and index.
Summary: Using one blackfooted penguin as an example, describes the birth, growth, and nurture of the species.
ISBN 0-531-15212-X—0-531-10988-7 (lib. bdg.)
1. Jackass penguin—Juvenile literature. [1. Jackass penguin. 2. Penguins.] I. Title.
QL696.S473P35   1991
598.4'41—dc20   90-13062 CIP AC

A baby penguin sleeps inside its egg. Curled into a neat ball, its tiny body floats in a cushion of watery fluid.

The penguin egg sits in an **incubator** at the New England Aquarium, keeping warm. It looks like a large, white chicken egg. For forty days and nights the baby penguin, called an **embryo,** has been growing inside. Once, its body was as small and bare as a lima bean. Now it almost fills the egg. Black feathers cover all but the little penguin's beak and webbed feet.

Penguins at the New England Aquarium usually incubate their eggs and raise their young themselves, in burrows. A special spot of bare skin on a penguin's belly, called a **brood patch,** helps to keep eggs warm until they hatch. Both male and female penguins have brood patches. They take turns incubating their eggs and caring for their chicks once they hatch. Most penguins lay just one or two eggs at a time.

Soon after this egg was laid, an animal caretaker at the Aquarium removed it from its nest. By hatching it and others in an incubator, the Aquarium hopes to learn more about raising healthy penguin chicks.

Naturally, penguins get upset when an egg is taken from them. They attack intruders with their sharp bills. Dan, the penguins' head caretaker, put on thick gloves before he reached into one of the **burrows**. The pair of black-footed penguins inside guarded their egg. They snapped at Dan as though he were an egg thief.

In the wild, hungry gulls steal eggs from penguin nests. But Dan moved slowly, speaking to the penguins in a calm voice. He gently grasped their egg in his hand and wrapped it in a soft towel. Then he brought it to the incubator.

Blackfooted penguins usually lay a second egg a few days after the first one. The second egg will be left in the burrow for the penguin couple to hatch.

Now, the first egg is ready to hatch. It has been in the incubator for several weeks. The baby penguin inside has used up almost all of the egg's **yolk** for food. Soon it will need food from the world outside.

The egg moves slightly. Inside, the penguin pokes its beak through a thin skin into an air pocket. For the first time the baby penguin breathes air. Then it starts tapping. The penguin uses a small, sharp bump on its beak to crack the hard shell. This bump is called an **egg tooth**. The egg tooth will fall off in a few days, when the penguin no longer needs it.

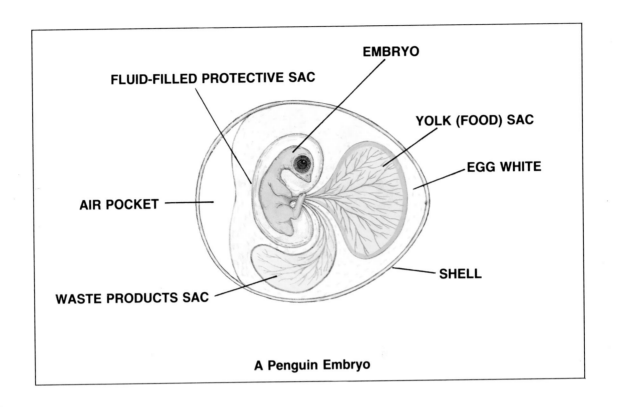

FLUID-FILLED PROTECTIVE SAC

EMBRYO

YOLK (FOOD) SAC

EGG WHITE

AIR POCKET

SHELL

WASTE PRODUCTS SAC

A Penguin Embryo

Soon a fine crack appears on the eggshell. Little by little, the baby penguin chips away. Finally, it punches a small hole right through. This is the **pip hole.**

Pipping is hard work. The penguin stops to rest, poking its little beak out through the pip hole. Suddenly, the beak opens. "Cheep! Cheep!" Out comes a sound like a squeak toy.

Normally, a baby bird continues pecking and resting, pecking and resting, until its egg cracks open. When it hatches, it is called a **chick.**

■ 8

Sometimes hatching takes a couple of days. But after two days, this little penguin is still in its egg. The penguin caretakers worry that it will need food soon. They decide to help it finish hatching.

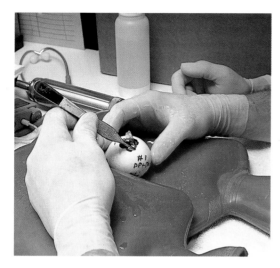
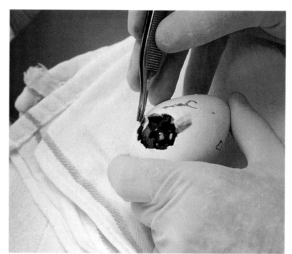
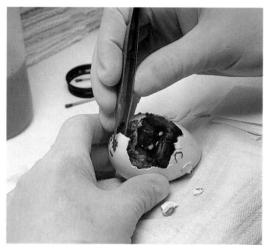

Using a pair of big tweezers, a caretaker named Greg taps the shell around the pip hole to make it bigger. Carefully, he peels away bits of eggshell and the protective skin underneath. The baby penguin is now chirping loudly and impatiently. It sounds like a robin.

Little by little the chips come off until finally, half the shell is gone. There, lying curled up in the other half, is the little penguin chick. It stretches out a tiny foot and already looks too big to have ever fitted in its egg.

Some penguin **hatchlings** are nearly bald, just like some human babies, but not this one. Its feathers, which look like fur, are soaking wet from the fluid that bathed the penguin in its egg.

Then Greg places the penguin chick in another incubator. A small fan blows its gray feathers until they fluff up soft and dry.

The animal caretaker won't be able to tell whether the penguin is male or female until after it has mated. Since it's easier to keep track of animals by calling them either "he" or "she," this one will be called "she" for now.

The Aquarium names this chick Pomona. She is a blackfooted penguin like her parents. Unlike some penguins that live in the snowy Antarctic, blackfoots nest on islands off the coast of South Africa, where the temperature is mild. Pomona is the name of one of these islands.

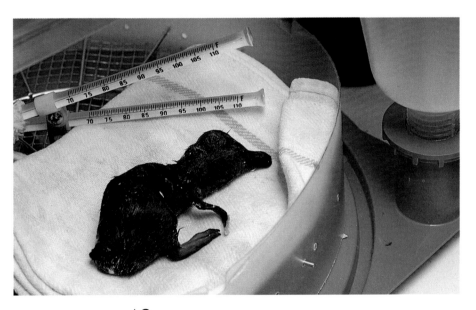

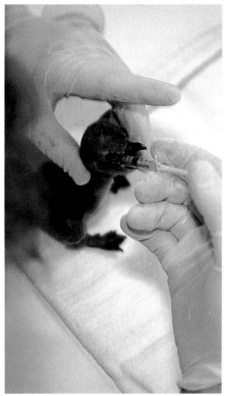

Like any baby, Pomona has a huge appetite. When she's not sleeping, she's wide awake and begging for food. The penguin caretakers make her a special kind of penguin baby food—cream of herring pudding. Pomona thinks it's tasty, and gobbles up six helpings a day.

Even with all that food, Pomona is still too weak to stand up or lift her head. She tries desperately, but collapses onto her blanket each time, exhausted.

Different kinds of baby birds develop at different rates. Some, like chickens, are very steady on their feet almost as soon as they hatch. Penguin hatchlings can take longer.

A toy penguin keeps Pomona company and gives her something soft to lean on. If she were in a nest with her parents, Pomona would snuggle close to them for warmth and comfort.

In the wild, penguins feed their hungry chicks by bringing up partially digested fish from their own stomachs. The chick reaches with its beak into its parent's open mouth to eat. Both penguin parents share the job of feeding their young.

To feed Pomona, the caretakers make a **V** with their fingers. The shape mimics a parent penguin's open mouth. As soon as Pomona feels the **V** around her beak, she opens her mouth up eagerly. The caretakers squeeze in the pudding through a syringe.

Every morning, Pomona is weighed on a little scale. She eats enormous amounts of food, two-thirds her body weight each day. When fully grown, blackfooted penguins weigh about 8 pounds (3.6 kg) and stand 12 to 18 inches (30.5 to 45.7 cm) tall.

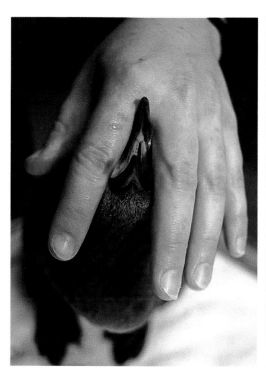

Pomona grows very fast, and gets a little stronger every day. Still a bit wobbly when she stands up, Pomona prefers to squat like a duck. But one day, she surprises her caretaker in the middle of a feeding. Pomona suddenly lifts herself up. With head high and **flippers** outstretched, she toddles across the counter at top speed.

Pomona has a new diet now—herring fillets. These are fish with the bones removed. She likes them even better than herring pudding. When she's bigger, Pomona will eat whole fish, bones and all. Penguins in the wild eat seafood, including fish, squid, and shrimplike animals called krill.

Pomona ruffles her soft gray feathers, which are called **baby down.** Penguin baby down is not waterproof. A downy penguin chick could drown if it went in the water because its soaked feathers would weigh it down.

All penguins eventually lose their baby down and grow new adult feathers. This is called **molting.** Penguins make their adult feathers waterproof by spreading oil on them with their beaks. The oil comes from a **gland** at the base of their tails.

Pomona begins to molt when she is a little over one month old. Molting makes her grumpy. She stands in a corner like a sack of flour, sometimes nipping at visitors. Molting probably feels uncomfortable. Sleek, dark feathers grow in, pushing out her fuzzy gray tufts. These new feathers overlap in thick layers. They will keep cold air and water away from Pomona's body.

With her new feathers, Pomona is no longer a chick. But she is still not quite an adult. She is called a **juvenile.** Juvenile blackfooted penguins are dark gray with off-white bellies. When Pomona molts again next year, she'll have the crisp black chest stripe, black face mask, and bright white belly of an adult blackfoot.

In her new waterproof coat, Pomona is ready to learn how to swim.
A caretaker named Heather carries her
to a small pool to practice. At first,
Heather holds Pomona under her belly
to let her feel the water. But Pomona
fidgets. Flippers flapping, she breaks
free and heads for the ramp. Some-
how, she scrambles out. Standing with
her back to the pool and dripping wet,
Pomona makes it clear that swimming
practice is over for today!

Heather takes Pomona to the pool
a few more times during the week.

Slowly, Pomona gets used to the water. Soon, she will be swimming underwater like other penguins.

Now Pomona is ready to swim in the main Aquarium pool. Twenty-three blackfooted penguins, including her parents and grandparents, live here. Rockhopper penguins live here, too. They are about the same size as blackfoots, but they have yellow feather tufts over their beady red eyes, and no stripe or facemask. The Aquarium's rockhoppers come from Noir Island, Chile, and the South African coast.

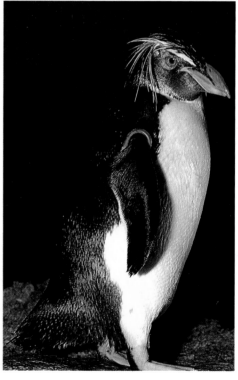

A caretaker named Chris takes Pomona for her first swim in the big pool. He makes sure she knows how to climb out onto the rocks. After several more short visits, Pomona is ready to stay in the pool overnight.

At first, Pomona paddles around shyly. Accidentally, she dunks her head and quickly pulls it out again. What was that?

■ 24

She ducks under the surface for another look, forgetting to be afraid. Sparkles and shadows ripple everywhere in dazzling shapes. Other penguins zip by with amazing speed. This is a whole new world! Penguins were *made* to fly underwater!

Flapping her wings excitedly, Pomona shoots forward under the water. She's flying!

Penguins' wings are called flippers. Instead of flying through air like other birds, penguins fly through water. Tapered at both ends like footballs, their bodies are streamlined for fast swimming.

Out on the rocks, the adult penguins don't want to have much to do with juveniles, especially newcomers like Pomona. They have already chosen their favorite island spots.

But there is another juvenile black-footed penguin in the pool named Benguela. Benguela is the name of the cold ocean current along the coast of South Africa where blackfooted penguins swim. In the wild, juvenile penguins tend to stick together in groups. Together, Benny and Pomona pick out their own tiny island to share while they're growing up.

AFTERWORD
THE PLIGHT OF THE PENGUIN

The number of blackfooted penguins that live in the wild is decreasing. Millions used to nest on the islands off the coast of South Africa. Today they number only in the thousands.

Over the centuries, several factors have caused this decline. Fifteenth-century European explorers killed huge numbers of penguins to feed crews aboard sailing ships. As European settlements grew in South Africa, people collected penguins eggs by the millions for food. Their special flavor made penguin eggs a gourmet item in restaurants. Commercial egg collecting went on until the late 1960s, when it was prohibited.

Not only were penguins and their eggs collected, but people took their homes as well. Blackfooted penguins nest in holes dug in dried bird manure, called guano. Guano makes a good fertilizer because it contains nitrogen, phosphorus, and other plant nutrients. Mounds of guano were collected for use in gardens, particularly during the 1800s.

Oil spills are a constant threat to the survival of blackfooted penguins. Past oil spills killed tens of thousands of blackfooted penguins around the southern tip of Africa. Future spills could wipe out those that remain.

Finally, the South African fishing industry harvests tons of fish every year from the penguins' feeding grounds. Fewer penguins can survive if their food supply continues to dwindle.

Blackfooted penguins raised in captivity are protected from these threats. As long as some of them live in places like the New England Aquarium, the future of this special bird will be a little bit safer.

GLOSSARY

Baby down (bay-bee down)—the fluffy feathers of a chick before the juvenile feathers grow in. In penguins, baby down is not waterproof.

Benguela (ben-GWAY-la)—the name of a cold ocean current flowing northward off the west coast of South Africa. It is home to the blackfooted penguin.

Brood patch—a bare spot of skin on a bird's belly used for keeping eggs and young warm

Burrow (BURR-oh)—the small hole or cave where a penguin pair nests

Chick—a newly hatched or young bird

Egg tooth—a hard, sharp bump on the beak of an unhatched bird, or the nose of an unhatched reptile, used to break open the eggshell

Embryo (EM-bree-oh)—a backboned animal in the early stages of development before it is born or hatched

Flippers (FLIP-ers)—the penguin's paddle-like wings, used for swimming

Gland—an organ that produces a substance that may be used by the body, such as oil or digestive fluids

Hatchling (HATCH-ling)—a newly hatched bird

Incubator (IN-cue-bait-or)—a special container for keeping eggs warm artificially until they hatch

Juvenile (JOO-vuh-nile)—a young bird that has shed its baby down but does not yet have the feathers of an adult

Molting (MOLE-ting)—the shedding of old feathers for new ones

Pip—to break open the shell of an egg in hatching

Pip hole—the small hole a chick makes in its egg when it begins hatching

Pomona (pah-MOAN-ah)—One of the islands off the South African coast where blackfooted penguins nest.

Yolk (YOKE)—the thick, usually golden yellow material that provides food for a very young animal.

SUGGESTED READING

Arnold, Caroline. **Penguin.** New York: William Morrow, 1988.

Bonners, Susan. **A Penguin Year.** New York: Delacorte Press, 1981.

Coldrey, Jenny. **Penguin.** New York: Andre Deutsch, 1984.

Hoffman, Mary. **Penguin.** Milwaukee: Raintree Publications, 1985.

Johnson, Sylvia. **Penguins.** Minneapolis: Lerner Publications Co., 1981.

Lepthien, Emile E. **Penguin.** San Francisco: Childrens Book Press, 1983.

Royston, Angela. **The Penguin.** New York: Franklin Watts, 1988.

Saintsing, David. **The World of Penguins.** Milwaukee: Gareth Stevens Inc., 1987.

Serventy, Vincent. **Penguin.** New York: Scholastic, Inc., 1986.

Stone, Lynn M. **The Penguins.** Mankato, Minnesota: Crestwood House, 1987.

Stonehouse, Bernard. **Penguins.** New York: McGraw-Hill Book Company, 1979.

Strange, Ian J. **Penguin World.** New York: Dodd, Mead & Company, 1981.

Tenaza, Richard. **Penguins.** New York: Franklin Watts, 1980.

Todd, Frank S. **The Sea World Book of Penguins.** New York: Harcourt Brace Jovanovich, Inc., 1981.

INDEX

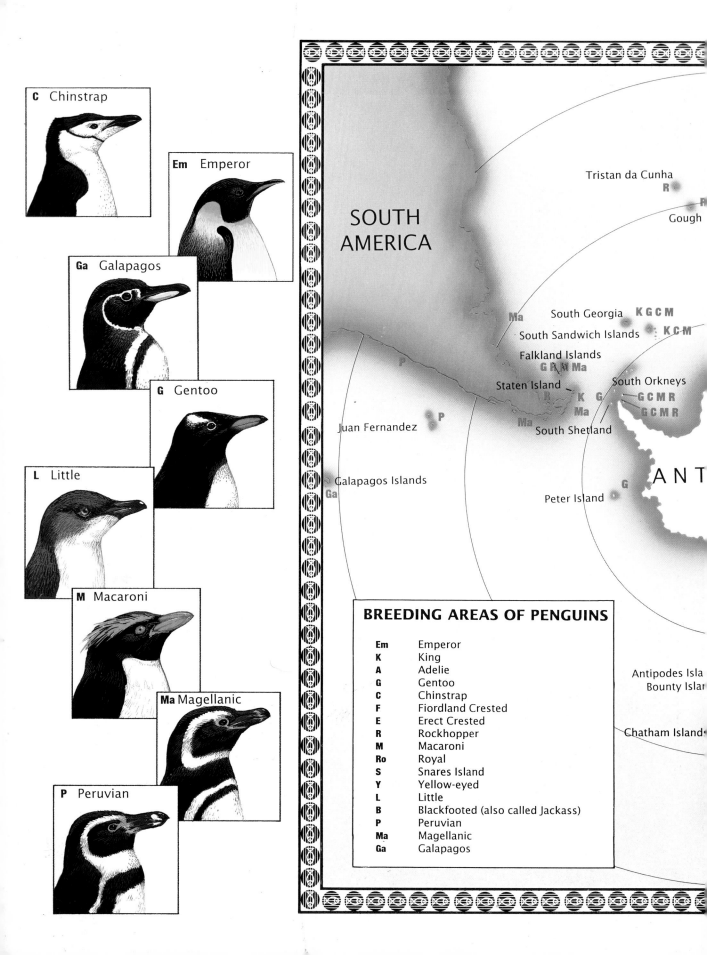

C Chinstrap

Em Emperor

Ga Galapagos

G Gentoo

L Little

M Macaroni

Ma Magellanic

P Peruvian

SOUTH
AMERICA

Tristan da Cunha · R

Gough · R

Ma · South Georgia · K G C M

South Sandwich Islands · K C M

Falkland Islands
G R M Ma

Staten Island · K G · South Orkneys
G C M R
G C M R

Ma · South Shetland

P · Juan Fernandez

P

Ma

Galapagos Islands
Ga

Peter Island · G

A N T

ANTipodes Isla
Bounty Islar

Chatham Island

BREEDING AREAS OF PENGUINS

Em	Emperor
K	King
A	Adelie
G	Gentoo
C	Chinstrap
F	Fiordland Crested
E	Erect Crested
R	Rockhopper
M	Macaroni
Ro	Royal
S	Snares Island
Y	Yellow-eyed
L	Little
B	Blackfooted (also called Jackass)
P	Peruvian
Ma	Magellanic
Ga	Galapagos